THE BALLAD OF
ABLE SEACAT SIMON
OF HMS AMETHYST

BY MARGARET MACDONALD
ILLUSTRATED BY BECKY BROWN

For Mary and Callum

Published in 2020 by Margaret Macdonald
Aberdeenshire, Scotland

Sixty per cent of all profits from each book
sold will be divided equally between the PDSA and
a children's charity

Typeset by Lumphanan Press
www.lumphananpress.co.uk

Illustrations by Becky Brown © 2020

Printed by The Gatehouse, Aberdeen

ISBN: 978-1-8382023-0-9

CONTENTS

Thank you to the PDSA and Lieutenant Commander Stewart Hett for allowing me to use their archive photos in this book.

Page 17   Photograph of Simon and crew on board HMS Amethyst. Courtesy of PDSA.

Page 21   Photograph of HMS Amethyst. Courtesy of PDSA.

Page 28   Photograph of damaged HMS Amethyst. Courtesy of Lieutenant Commander Stewart Hett.

Page 36   Photograph of HMS Amethyst's company marching through Plymouth – November 1949. Courtesy of Lieutenant Commander Stewart Hett.

Page 37   Photograph of Simon's PDSA Dickin Medal. Courtesy of the PDSA.

INTRODUCTION

Simon 1947–1949

Simon's story is TRUE and shows how the most unlikely of creatures can become a hero when they are needed.

Simon started life as a stray kitten living on the docks of Stonecutters Island, Hong Kong. In March 1948, 17-year-old Ordinary Seaman George Hickinbottom came across the homeless Simon and smuggled the cat on to his ship, HMS Amethyst. Black cats are considered to be good luck by sailors and Simon quickly became a valuable member of the ship's crew by working as a rat-catcher, which helped protect the food stores.

This ballad tells the story of the twists and turns that Simon's life took. These led him to different countries and through many dangers, eventually taking him to England where he received three medals for bravery! Simon was awarded the Naval General Service Medal, The Blue Cross Medal and The Dickin Medal, the last of which is the highest British honour for animal displays of bravery in battle. Other recipients of The Dickin Medal include messenger pigeons, dogs and horses. To this day, Simon is the only cat to be awarded The Dickin Medal.

Simon was placed in quarantine when he arrived in England but sadly died on November 28th 1949. He was buried with full naval honours in Ilford, Essex, alongside other animal heroes.

There is a lot of available information about Simon, the crew and HMS Amethyst. A movie called "The Yangtze Incident" depicts their story. Online you can find first-hand accounts from crew members with live recordings of the ship's journey back to Britain and footage of Simon. I have included links to some of these films on my author's website which you can access at:

www.margaretmacdonaldauthor.com

Or by scanning the QR code below:

Let us all keep in mind the brave men, women and animals who serve their countries and pass their stories on to future generations.

Lest We Forget

GLOSSARY

Bilges – Lowest space or compartment of a ship where water collects.

Bosun – The senior crewman responsible for equipment on the deck of a ship.

Bow – The front section of a ship.

Bridge – Area at the top of a ship from where the Captain commands.

The Dickin Medal – The highest award for animal courage in battle. The medal was created in 1943 by Maria Dickin, who founded the charity the People's Dispensary for Sick Animals (PDSA).

Gallantry – Showing bravery and courage.

Galley – The area of the ship where food is prepared and cooked.

HMS Amethyst – His/Her Majesty's Ship (HMS). The Amethyst was a warship used by the British Royal Navy between 1943-1957.

HMS Consort – The Royal Navy warship used to guard the British Embassy at Nanking in April 1949. At that time, Nanking was the capital of China. Now the capital is Beijing.

Mariner – A person who works on a ship.

Monsoon – A seasonal weather pattern, characterised by very heavy rainfall in the Pacific, West African Atlantic and Indian Ocean.

Quarantine – The period of time an animal (or human) newly arrived in the UK is kept away from others to prevent the spread of diseases from other countries.

Salute – To greet with an expression of respect.

Shrapnel – Metal fragments scattered by exploding bombs.

Splice the Mainbrace – An order given by the Royal Navy to give the crew an extra ration of rum.

Stern – The back section of a ship.

Typhoon – Very strong winds that occur in the China Sea.

The Yangtze Incident – A historic event which involved HMS Amethyst and other Royal Navy ships on the Yangtze river for three months during the Chinese Civil War in the summer of 1949.

The Yangtze River – The longest river in the world to flow entirely within one country (China). It is 3,915 miles long (6,300 kilometres).

I am Able Seacat Simon.
I had no home or name.
The tale I'd like to share with you
Is how I rose to fame.

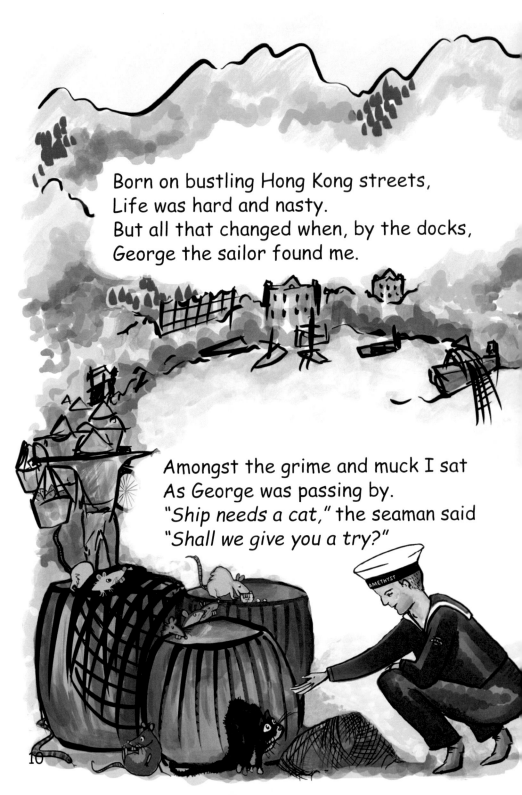

Born on bustling Hong Kong streets,
Life was hard and nasty.
But all that changed when, by the docks,
George the sailor found me.

Amongst the grime and muck I sat
As George was passing by.
"Ship needs a cat," the seaman said
"Shall we give you a try?"

10

He carried me inside his shirt
Aboard the *Amethyst*.
I felt a kindness in his touch,
No impulse to resist.

All things on board were strange to me:
So hard to live near men.
What was safe or perilous?
I had to learn again.

I didn't have my sea legs;
The motion made me sick.
The cure was lots of fresh salt air.
George said: "You've come on quick."

In days and weeks I felt better,
Grew fond of the scents and sounds.
The scrumptious food had made me strong
So I began my rounds.

By day, I stalked about the ship
From bow to bridge to stern,
Locating where to find the rats.
By night, I would return.

I'd snatch them in the bilges,
The galley and the slop,
Guzzling up the sailors' grub.
My job? To make them stop.

Daily treats I'd have from Cook,
Though he was always busy.
One day he spied a brazen rat
While seated on the privy!

Cook roared "That rat's ENORMOUS.
A Rodent King for sure."
Once more into the fray I went.
That pest plagued loos no more.

I loved the Captain best of all:
He had the softest bed.
I gave him most of what I caught.
"A gift for you," I said.

He chose to call me Simon,
No more a nameless waif.
"A First Class Ratter, that's what you are."
My place on board was safe.

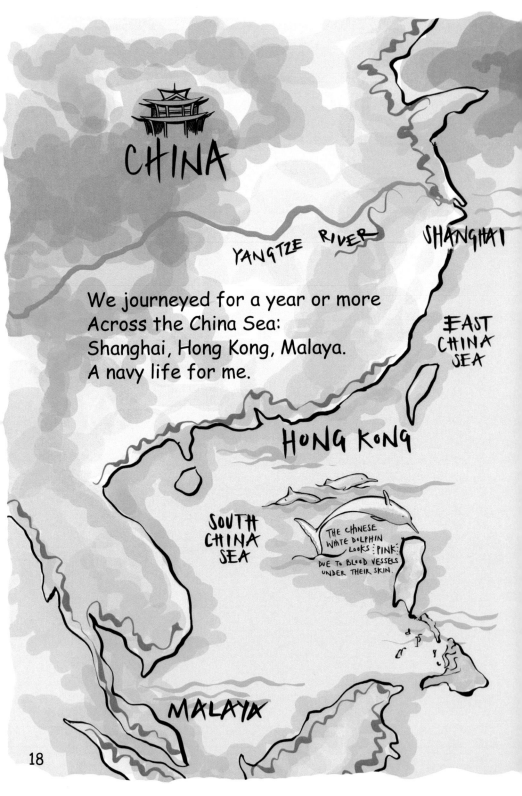

CHINA

YANGTZE RIVER

SHANGHAI

EAST CHINA SEA

We journeyed for a year or more
Across the China Sea:
Shanghai, Hong Kong, Malaya.
A navy life for me.

HONG KONG

SOUTH CHINA SEA

THE CHINESE WHITE DOLPHIN LOOKS PINK DUE TO BLOOD VESSELS UNDER THEIR SKIN.

MALAYA

MANY SPECIES OF WHALE ARE FOUND IN THE SEAS AROUND CHINA ... THIS INCLUDES THE BLUE WHALE, THE WORLD'S LARGEST MAMMAL

Typhoon winds brought crashing waves,
Stirred tornadoes in the sea.
In the distance, pirate ships
Would spot our flag and flee.

Whales' tails smacked the water;
Sea birds flew past with a *swish*.
Dolphins pranced beside us
Chasing shoals of flying fish.

Congested, clamouring harbours;
Sweet smells, sweat and spice;
Night skies jewelled with twinkling stars:
A life in paradise.

FLYING FISH

CHINA

SHANGHAI

NANKING
(NOW NANJING)

WANHSIEN
(NOW WANZHOU)

HANKOW
(NOW WUHAN)

INCHANG
(NOW YICHANG)

YANGTZE RIVER

Then one day came an order:

MAKE ALL SPEED TO NANKING.

RELIEVE HMS CONSORT.

EMBASSY NEEDS GUARDING.

At this time in China
There raged a civil war.
Our ship risked being fired at
By guns from either shore.

Flags were draped along our hull;
All were vigilant;
Unaware we were heading for
The Yangtze Incident.

On that April morning,
In Nineteen Forty-Nine,
We steamed up the mighty river;
I felt tingles down my spine.

The Bosun shouted orders.
Trouble was in the air.
Sailors' feet were running.
There was action everywhere.

BANG

From nowhere came explosions,
Bomb blasts and flashing lights,
Blazing fires with choking smoke,
Excruciating sights.

In the fight, we ran aground,
Stuck fast into the mud.
Hit by flying shrapnel,
I fell down with a thud.

I woke to find my fur burned;
Pain racked my legs and hips;
A buzzing sound rang in my ears;
Blood was on my lips.

Seamen were lying wounded;
The mood was one of dread;
The ship was badly damaged;
Good chums were hurt or dead.

The doctor helped the injured
Then nursed my cuts and pain.
For days, still scared, I hid myself
Till I felt brave again.

To lift the sailors' spirits
I slept in the sick bay
And let the mariners stroke me
To calm them as they lay.

They spoke about their loved ones,
The folk they'd left at home.
Together we healed as comrades,
Afraid to be alone.

27

For months we could go nowhere:
Paradise seemed long ago.
Food, supplies and medicines,
All were running low.

Any ship sent to rescue us
Came in gunfire range.
The Skipper had to sit things out
Until there was a change.

MOSQUITOS ARE SMALL INSECTS. THE FEMALES BITE AND SUCK BLOOD. SOME MOSQUITOS SPREAD DISEASE.

Monsoon brought mosquitos;
Muggy nights were hot.
The rascal rats grew bolder.
I vowed to catch the lot!

From hunting rats to soothing crew,
I helped each man aboard.
I was now ranked *"Able Seacat!"*
AND promised an award!

At last a typhoon out at sea
Increased the river's height.
The Captain quickly hatched a plan
To steam away that night.

Without a pilot to guide us through,
We trusted Skipper's savvy
To safely steer the *Amethyst*
Down the river Yangtze.

THE SHIP'S WHEEL
IS USED TO STEER
A SHIP'S COURSE.
IT IS CONNECTED
TO THE RUDDER
WHICH CONTROLS
THE DIRECTION
OF A SHIP
THROUGH THE
WATER.

All through the night guns blasted out
Along the northern shore.
The ship *s-h-u-d-d-e-r-e-d and j-u-d-d-e-r-e-d*
But we were hit no more.

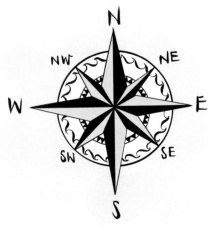

A COMPASS IS USED FOR NAVIGATION. IT HAS A MAGNETISED POINTER WHICH SHOWS THE DIRECTION OF MAGNETIC NORTH.

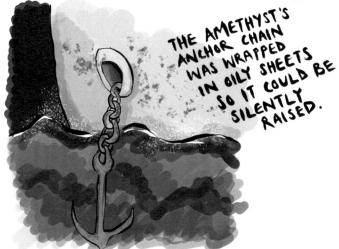

THE AMETHYST'S ANCHOR CHAIN WAS WRAPPED IN OILY SHEETS SO IT COULD BE SILENTLY RAISED.

At length we reached safe harbour
And whoops of joy were heard.
"Splice the mainbrace," the Captain said.
I lapped up milk and purred.

Our ordeals now behind us,
We headed out to sea,
To a place the crew called Plymouth.
They spoke the name with glee.

Our voyage was a long one,
With many stops en route.
At each port people cheered us,
Horns tooted in salute.

PLYMOUTH PRESS

November 1st 1949

On reaching Plymouth, England,
Crowds as far as you could see
Waved Union Jacks in greeting
The ship, the crew **AND ME!**

They said "Simon, you'll be given
A medal of bravery!
You went beyond the call of duty.
You've made naval history."

"Never has The Dickin Medal
Been given to a cat.
For months you were our comfort
AND hunted every rat!"

Amidst these celebrations
Came something unforeseen,
When the crew began to mention
A place called "QUARANTINE".

If I'd understood their meaning
I would have gone astray.
Once more life changed beyond compare
When a **VAN** drove me away!

Kept in a dismal building
For what seemed like an age,
So different from the ship I loved,
My home was now a cage.

My sailor friends would visit me,
Sit chatting on a stool.
But then they'd leave without me
Because that was the rule.

I dreamt about them often and
Our ship in Plymouth's bay.
I longed to be on board her
To taste the tangy spray.

One day I woke and couldn't rise,
Too weak to leave my bed.
An Angel came and lifted me.
"Come with me, Simon," he said.

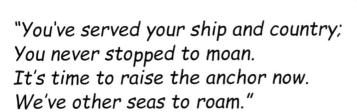

*"You've served your ship and country;
You never stopped to moan.
It's time to raise the anchor now.
We've other seas to roam."*

I am Able Seacat Simon,
A cut above the best.
Today, I'll cross the Rainbow Bridge
To start a brand new quest.

You know what they say? Cats have nine lives...

INTERNATIONAL CODE OF SIGNALS

Challenge:
Can you draw your name using the flags?

ACKNOWLEDGEMENTS

There is truth in the African proverb "It takes a village to raise a child". The statement is equally legitimate for writing a book. Even this short story benefited from the help of family and friends.

Thanks are due to:

My mother-in-law Mary, who introduced me to the story of Simon.

My dear husband Graham and daughter Layla for encouraging my artistic talent and keeping family meltdowns to a minimum!

My sisters Pauline and Deirdre, both primary school teachers, for understanding, as best as anyone can, the minds of children.

Artist Becky Brown, for her inventive illustrations www.facebook.com/theillustratedtreeco

My friend Jill for allowing me to ruin girls' nights in together by focusing on this book!

My mentor John Bolland, for facilitating my creative writing: aviewfromthelonggrass.com

My friends Penny and David for picking up on everything I forgot from English classes!

The PDSA team, particularly Katrina Gilbert, Legacy and Community Fundraiser, for believing in this book enough to encourage its production and for providing archive photographs for use in the book.

Huntly Writers for supporting me as a new writer.

Lieutenant Commander K. Stewart Hett, MBE, RN, (deceased), a former member of the *Amethyst* crew, who supplied archive photographs.

Last but not least, Molinda, who provided me with the book that helped me write this book!

There are also numerous others to whom I am grateful to for their support and contributions. I hope I have expressed it to each of you enough to confidently use the phrase 'you know who you are'! Believe me when I say that your help has been invaluable.

MARGARET MACDONALD

Photo by "Althea Dreams of Photography"

Margaret Macdonald was born in Colombo, Sri Lanka and moved to London in 1959. Since 1985, she has lived in North East Scotland, where she studied, raised her children and worked. Margaret is a qualified social worker, mediator and trainer. She discovered Simon's story through her mother-in-law Mary and was inspired to write a rhyming tale for children about this extraordinary cat. *The Ballad of Able Seacat Simon of HMS Amethyst* is her first children's book.

As a self-published author, it is really important for Margaret to receive feedback. She would be extremely grateful if you would take a couple of minutes to review her book on Amazon so that more people can learn about and enjoy Simon's story.